"POWER-TO-BECOME"
BOOK-PAK SERIES • BOOK TWO

A MAN'S CONFIDENCE

*A Study of How Men
Become Confident in Life
Through Mastering Guilt*

by JACK

A Man's Confidence

Published by Living Way Ministries
14300 Sherman Way
Van Nuys, CA (USA) 91405-2499
(818)779-8180 • (800) 776-8180

ISBN 0-916847-11-X
Printed in the United States of America

*This message was originally brought
at The Church On The Way.*

*It has since been edited and revised
for publication by Pastor Hayford,
in partnership with Pastor Bob Anderson,
Director of Pastoral Relations.*

*The audio cassette of this message
(#1982)
may be purchased from:*

*Living Way Ministries
14300 Sherman Way
Van Nuys, CA 91405*

TABLE OF CONTENTS

Beloved, if our heart does not condemn us, we have confidence toward God.

And whatever we ask we receive from Him, because we keep His commandments and do those things that are pleasing in His sight.   1 John 3:21-22

The Lord is merciful and gracious, slow to anger, and abounding in mercy. He will not always strive with us, nor will He keep His anger forever.

He has not dealt with us according to our sins, nor punished us according to our iniquities.   For as the heavens are high above the earth, so great is His mercy toward those who fear Him;

As far as the east is from the west, so far has He removed our transgressions from us. As a father pities his children, so the Lord pities those who fear Him.   For He knows our frame; He remembers that we are dust.   Psalm 103:8-14

CHAPTER ONE:

RECOVERING
CONFIDENCE

The moon was just rising over the college campus, casting long shadows which slanted across the brick staircase where I stood, dejectedly looking down the curved pathway to the courtyard below. I was in my first year of studies for the ministry–dedicated to everything I believed God wanted me to be. But I was defeated!

The immediate reason for my depression was a very recent instance of failure–of yielding to besetting sin which dogged my path and recurrently struck condemnation to my soul.

As I sat down on the casement beside the stairs, I brooded over my failure. I wasn't feeling self-pitying, I was simply beaten by my own humanness, and trying to figure out how to square things with God. I had mixed feelings. I'd failed often enough in this same way that I felt dishonest coming to God again with my sorry tale of stumbling.

It was a Sunday evening, and the campus was empty. My fellow students were either out ministering someplace, or worshiping at the campus church not more than a hundred yards from where I sat. But I was on the outside–and felt it deeply; not being outside of church or my circle of friends, so much as *well* outside a circle of *confidence*. I *did* know I was saved, at least I supposed that hadn't changed, since I knew that God is long on grace. But what I didn't know was how to shake the weight of guilt on my soul; a heaviness that hung like metal weights all over me, for I felt unworthy even to *ask* for forgiveness. When you've asked to be forgiven for the same thing over and over, you begin to wonder if God will even take you seriously if you ask again.

I was yet to enter into a fuller grasp of God's truth which would eventually insulate me against this kind of attack. It's that wilting assault on the soul which seems to beset hosts of Christians who are just as sincere as I was that evening, but who haven't found the key of confidence in their relationship with God. But something was about to happen. In His mercy, God was about to whisper to me by His Holy Spirit; to whisper a set of words from His Word which would become the *real* beginning of an abiding spiritual confidence I would eventually come to learn to live in.

It's still an unforgotten moment.

Though decades have passed since I sat there in that campus setting, my soul wearied to near despair, I still recall the sound of the Voice which spoke to my heart–timeless words you can find engraved in His Eternal Word:

> *"If we confess our sin, He is faithful and just to forgive us our sin, and to cleanse us from all unrighteousness."* 1 John 1:9

It wasn't as though I had not heard those words before; indeed, I had memorized them as a child. But there is a world of difference between reading, hearing, or remembering a set of words, and having them *revealed* to your spirit! And that's what happened.

Suddenly, it was as though the moonlight swelled to sunlight, as though chains snapped and a helmet of lead was removed from my mind. I KNEW God had heard my request for forgiveness. I KNEW He did not view me as a minced-minded compromiser. I KNEW He was both forgiving me and freeing me. I KNEW I was being–*that moment*–cleansed and released.

I KNEW IT!!

And my heart rose with a joy which seemed to leap inside me, as despair, defeat, and depression melted before the power of

God's Word which had just been made gloriously alive by the Holy Spirit's voice to my soul. It was a release and rejoicing which I earnestly pray might be yours; might be the portion of any and every believer who has ever been badgered by the crushing weight of condemnation's force.

As I stood from where I had been sitting on the brick casement, I virtually felt I could fly. And the most gratifying thing about that whole encounter with God's redeeming, releasing truth was the overwhelming sense of *confidence* which possessed my heart.

> *"Beloved, if our heart does not condemn us, we have confidence toward God."* 1 John 3:21

Confidence.
    The settled peace of certainty
    in the soul.
Confidence.
    The knowledge that you can
    achieve a goal.
Confidence.
    The inner sense that all is
    right and well.
Confidence.
    The breath of heav'n that snuffs
    the fires of hell.

The Right "Stuff"

This book has to do with a man's confidence *toward God*. It's based on the proven fact that until *that* arena of confidence is secured, all other efforts at *self*-secured confidence will inevitably prove inadequate. We're all creatures who have been brought into being with a dual capacity for life–both physical and spiritual. Any effort at treating life on half its terms is doomed. You and I must deal with our *spiritual* base of confidence first, or our other realms of supposed strength are without the "stuff" that makes life work–and *last*. A mound can be built of sand and stones, mixed with water, and a sandcastle erected with temporary splendor. But without the ingredient of concrete mixed in, the sand and stone will only last until they meet the rain, wind, or waves. And in the same way, the *spiritual* facet of a man's nature must be mixed *in* (not mixed up!). Only the integration of spiritual understanding–proportionately fit into the whole of all the other components which constitute a person's life–his duties, family, vocational goals, interests, and education–can bring a solid substance to life.

In our book-to-book studies for men, our target is to find the way to "mix in" the solidifying "stuff" of spiritual reality, so that every man, any man–YOU!–can cultivate that balance in life which gives the proper place to the spiritual aspect of your personality. Confidence in the spiritual realm is not readily achieved. This is because everything about attaining spiritual confidence is the reverse of the way most of us have gained confidence in other areas of our lives.

Usually, we men gain confidence through what we *achieve*.

Recognition.

Athletics.

Education.

Ownership.

Clothes.

Competition.

Conquest.

And on and on.

Earth-level confidence rises when successes are achieved and usually diminishes when failure impacts or the unexpected overthrows our best-laid plans.

An anticipated sale collapses.

An athlete's musculature is damaged.

A planned marriage is called off.

A promising investment turns to nothing.

It's a mere truism, but it deserves repeating: "Success" is only as long as success lasts. And when success comes to its end–even if it's been lifelong–*every* man ultimately has to come to terms with the spiritual aspect of his being: his relationship with God.*

Defining "Confidence"

There's where confidence finds its base–its foundation–and that provides a beginning. But how do we *build* on that foundation when our own humanness seems to fail and our confidence for growth seems shaken? To answer, let's first establish the definition of what we mean by "confidence." Let's open the dictionary a minute.

---

* In the back of this book, I've included a few words of guidance for anyone who may not have established a beginning point–a "newborn" point of life in knowing the Lord, God Almighty. Take time here–right now–if you haven't found THE KEY TO LIFE yet; for coming to know Jesus Christ, the Son of God, is the beginning place for attending to the spiritual part of your nature. Going back to the early sand-stone-cement analogy, the place you go to "bring it all together" and to "make it stick," is to the Cross of Christ, in faith and to your knees in prayer with humility before your Creator. But let me proceed now, on the assumption that you, Sir, have begun your life in Christ.

The word "confidence" has four essential uses or applications:

1. Confidence refers to "firm belief, trust, reliance."

2. Confidence refers to "the fact of being or feeling certain."

3. Confidence refers to "the belief in one's own abilities."

4. Confidence refers to "a relationship of trust in secrecy."

Impressive by any standard of analysis is that the *first* definition which asserts "belief, trust, reliance" is not only primary and foundational. It's exactly the real and the only path to a *lasting* confidence–the eternal kind. And look at those other three parts, and see how all secondary meanings of the word depend upon WHERE and IN WHOM you place your *first* point of confidence. *All* "feeling certain," *all* "belief in your ability," and *all* "trusting relationships" stem from the fountainhead of well-placed confidence. For a man to have abiding, transcending confidence, his relationship with God must become one of solid assurance and unshakable stability.

But how many forces war against that kind of relationship?

TALK ABOUT IT! Chapter questions to explore with a friend.

1. What are several false foundations upon which we men sometimes build our confidence?

2. What are four essential definitions or applications of confidence in a man's life?

3. Tell how you, in recent years, have transferred your confidence from a false foundation to one that is valid and biblically based.

CHAPTER TWO:

THE CRIPPLING EFFECTS OF CONDEMNATION

Condemnation is exactly that: it's *"crippling!"* It reduces a person to a stumbling, uncertain pathway in his walk with God. Under condemnation:

- There is no joy;

- Spiritual vision is clouded;

- Holy motivation is sucked empty; and

- Living for God can become a fearful pilgrimage of uncertainty, pain, and exhaustion.

The New Testament Greek word for "condemnation" is *katakrinō,* meaning "judgment coming down on." It strongly conveys the idea of a person being *brought down by that which is against them.* How perfectly that describes the feelings experienced by a person as the result of feeling condemnation. And it's a tragic non-necessity: nobody needs to feel condemnation if he knows the truth.

I want to pass on the secret to triumph

over condemnation. Because of what I have witnessed condemnation do in my own life, and what I know it can do in yours as well, I want to partner with you to assure mastery over this monster.

It's of more than passing or merely personal importance that condemnation be whipped. There are three specific negative effects that condemnation has on a person. The first is:

1. *Condemnation shakes our assurance toward God.*

Shaken assurance. It's a kind of spiritual/emotional drain-off. It deadens the soul's sensitivities. Instead of singing:

> *"Blessed Assurance, Jesus is Mine,*
> *Oh what a foretaste of glory divine";*

Have you ever felt like grinding out:

> *"Shaken assurance, Jesus ain't mine,*
> *Oh what a sick taste of hell's lies and*
> *mine."*

Assurance can be shaken so unpredictably. I dare say that *everyone* reading my words has had the experience. You wake up one morning, and there it is—for no apparent reason. Unpredictably, suddenly, without explanation, you climb out of bed feeling a heaviness in your soul.

Your thoughts begin to percolate: "Hey,

man! What did I do wrong? I feel like God's left me. He must be really ticked off!" It might be overcast outside, but whether it is or not, it is in your soul–and you *know* that something *must* be wrong: "Heaven's dark. Situation's bleak. I'm dead meat, spiritually."

And I've found when gloom-clouds gather and confidence flees, very soon you'll also hear a sly voice whispering to your soul; listing at least a half dozen reasons why you deserve to be feeling this way.

It's not the voice of God.

No, Sir. It's a self-appointed representative from hell who has swaggered into the room and begun to reel off "helpful suggestions"; arriving to "clear up" any mystery as to *why* you feel unholy, unwelcomed by God; why you feel unfit to serve Him.

"Aha! There's no doubt about it!" hisses the vindictive intruder. "That prideful attitude you allowed when driving home yesterday–it angered God! And don't forget, you didn't put money in that homeless person's basket at the supermarket! You know the Word: 'Whatever you've done to the least of the brethren, you've done to Jesus'! You heartless pig!"

But the Bible unmasks this intruder: he is our Adversary, the devil! (1 Peter 5:8). The Scriptures call him "the accuser of the brethren" (Rev. 12:10), and he takes detailed notes on every point of our human vulnerability, waiting for the most opportune moment to make his recitations. And brother, whether it's the devil or our own minds harking back to our failures, have you found what I have? *The most frustrating thing about it is, his accusations seem so disgustingly accurate!* Every pinprick of hell, every argument of my mind–they both tell me things that are *true*! "You did that! You failed here! You know what you thought! And *God doesn't like that*. It's small wonder you *feel* so crummy, man. You *are* crummy!"

Satan will even use Scripture against you. He'll proof-text his accusations with mastery. He did while tempting Jesus in the wilderness, so don't be surprised if he attempts the same with you!

Or if the whole truth won't work, he'll try half-truths. Or gross exaggeration. And if you've gained strength to resist in one area and remain confident in the face of condemnation, the hosts of hell assigned to your case will go to 'plan B.' Or 'plan C.' Hell's minions are tireless in trying every possible avenue of assault, hoping you'll "buy" into their condemnation council. The enemy will be satisfied to establish *any* degree of condemnation into which he can escort you. And of course, the worse, the better. It may be anywhere from feeling: "Oh God, I feel I'm a damned soul–lost forever; I've committed the Unpardonable Sin"; to your simply feeling, "Well, today's 'shot!' I'm so 'out-of-sync' with God's best plans for me, I'm as useless to Him as a brass door knocker! Maybe some other day I'll 'count' for Him. Some other time, but not today." Wherever you may find yourself on the scale of condemnation it makes little difference, because at any point it shakes confidence of our acceptability to God.

2. Condemnation cripples our confidence in daily living.

The Bible reveals God's desire to give us confidence in many ways. For one, when he begins His work in us, He promises that He'll continue it until Jesus Christ comes.

> ". . . Being confident of this very thing, that He who has begun a good work in you will complete it until the day of Jesus Christ." Philippians 1:6

He also says He is committed to completing everything involving me and my development.

> "The Lord will perfect that which concerns me; Your mercy, O Lord, endures forever; do not forsake the works of Your hands." Psalm 138:8.

But all such precious, dynamic words

from heaven tend to fall on a numb soul when condemnation has begun its work. That's because condemnation tends to "anesthetize" us–to blur or blind our sight, dull our sense of the truth that would otherwise liberate us. When condemnation clouds hang low, you can't seem to perceive God's truth as you normally would. You become spiritually hazy–can't see straight. As a result, though you launch into a new day, you feel defective even before you start; feeling anything except certainty that today is the Lord's, and it's going to be a good day.

The soul freshness wilts. The machinery of your spirit feels "gunked up." "Now that I think about it," your mind argues, "this is all probably something I deserve." And the case seems closed, even though it's argued on the basis of something that happened: "When was it, now? About five weeks ago? Five days? Five hours?" Although, "I think I asked God to forgive that," I still conclude, "Well, I *deserve* to feel crummy anyway. I *deserve* the guilt I feel."

And brother, as certain as the "just deserts" may be if you measure them on the scale of *human* justice–God has intended something for us that's arranged on a different basis. It's called "our redemption in Christ!" and in that circle of grace there are facts and promises the precise *opposite* of what we judge ourselves to deserve. But before we look at God's "better idea," let me agree with one thing. If you or I are only judging what we deserve on the terms of any program of legal justice *outside* Christ, then I'll agree: we *do* deserve a bad day; we *do* deserve the absence of God's presence; we *do* deserve the removal of confidence. Yessir! In fact, to put it as a blunt bottom line: we both *deserve* to go to hell!

-IF the ground we stand on is devoid of the blood stains of Jesus;

-IF we stand on the grounds of God's law and that alone. And,

-IF the scope of our self-assessment is based strictly on the sweat and merit of our performance, outside of divine grace–

If *these* are the parameters which govern our feeling right toward God and good about ourselves, then *yes*, we *deserve* to feel condemned. When we surrender to our feelings on the terms of such human reasoning, rather than submit in faith to the truth of God's Word, we're destined for futility.

The fastest we will ever ascend in spiritual confidence will be a slow crawl. The highest we'll rise will only be a slight incline gained, from the pit of our own unworthiness and condemnation to an earth-level limitation of self-generated, self-achieved "confidence."

This syndrome is so common, this tendency of succumbing to feeling totally disqualified, yet it's so seldom admitted. And when this terrible sense of evaporated certainty for ministry occurs, look what happens. My confidence toward *God*, my confidence in His work in my *life*, my confidence for what *I'm* to be that day, and my confidence for touching other *people* with spiritual power–it's *all* just had the Rototiller of condemnation chew gutters of mud through what should have been a garden of fruitfulness. At the very least, we feel demoted–notched well below the "Society-of-Saints-Qualified-to-Minister-Effectively." And this syndrome hangs on. That dark cloud can rise in ugliness anytime. It happens to all of us. And it happens often and will recur until we learn to deal with condemnation effectively. But there is an answer for a man's confidence toward God.

The solution is the truth of God's mighty Word: "In Your light we see *light* (for) . . . the entrance of Your Word gives *light*" (Psalm 6:9; 119:30). Hear it! The fountain of life-giving, truth-shedding-light is *only* in the Word of God, and in Its light we can be permanently led out and kept free of condemnation's clutches. So having identified this darksome monster, and the way it undercuts our assurance, confidence, and ministry, let's open the portals of *Light*. Darkness, shadows, and gloom of soul can

This level of confidence, based on efforts at reinstatement through a desperate groping for self-merit–for *anything* to justify ourselves before God–is totally fruitless. Yet, how many succumb to inner thinking somewhat like the following?

> *"I'd ask God to help me, but I feel like I fumbled so many times that I'll just, sort of, work my way through <u>this</u> day, and then see how I do. By the end of the day, maybe I'll have racked up some merit points and I'll feel better about asking God to accept me."*

And suppose you *do* do better that day. What then?

Will you come to God and say, "Lord, now that You've seen how really hard I've tried, could I negotiate with You on the basis of my merit points I think I've earned?" Will you recite your accomplishments, and conclude, "So, Lord, I think because I did so much better today, it seems now–at least I feel better thinking so–that maybe *I* deserve *You* to do something for *me* now. (Pause) I DID do better today, didn't I, God?"

But brother, that system doesn't hold an ounce of weight or contain a grain of truth. In the terms of Scripture, it's blind, barren, and worst of all, hopeless. Yet it *is* the way our minds work, isn't it? Sure it is! And it's cockeyed!!

If either of us is determined to live in the realm of self-gained-merit to find spiritual confidence, it's going to be a very long, wearing trip, because to do so means we'll be functioning in the "deficit economy" of human effort. But if we choose to move into the dimension of what God Himself has provided for us in Jesus Christ, then an entirely new arena of possibility opens to us, because *there*-in Christ-is an economy of infinite resource. Our Lord Jesus has *provided* and Father God has *secured* something for us which we could never afford to acquire on our own. *It's the very righteousness of God Himself,* and we'll look at more on that later.

But first look at the third and last of the things we're seeing that condemnation does to torment people. Along with shaken assurance and crippled confidence,

3. Condemnation evaporates our certainty for ministry.

This third crippling effect of condemnation pinches off God's life flow through us to others. Have you experienced that condition I described-waking up, feeling crummy, facing the day with a defeated disposition: "Just gonna have to stumble through this one"? And what happens?

The day begins, and you've no sooner walked into the office, onto the campus, or got onto the job, when a brother in Christ comes up to you and says, "Boy, am I glad to see you. Listen, man. I'm really having a problem, and I sure need you to pray with me. Could we do that now, or later today?" What do you feel like saying?

"Forget it!"

Naturally, we'd never *say that*, but it's exactly the way we feel. At least *I* have, haven't you? The impression instantly flashes inside your soul, which, if put int words, goes something like: "Me, pray? H Listen, buddy-rather than *me* pray for yo let me tell you the best thing you could do yourself: get as far away from me as you c because you'll be better off the further go! If you want to get something from (put space between me and you. I'm a (stump: a walking spiritual vacuum."

Sound familiar? Such thoughts because you feel disqualified.

"Ministry? Me?"

You feel even if you *were* to pray person, the words would bounce your face; hollow words from the spiritual non-entity, empty pray nothing of substance or worth, com words which are a mockery, voi spiritual confidence-a dynamic c you so deeply sense is missing. ' gonna happen through me! I'm be set running–scattered like night before dawn–when we know how to turn that light on.

TALK ABOUT IT! Chapter questions to explore with a friend.

1. What are three specific negative effects that condemnation has on a person?

2. What are several ways by which we try to justify ourselves before God?

3. Can you share any experience in which you felt hindered–due to condemnation–while trying to minister to another person? How did you overcome it?

CHAPTER THREE:

DISCERNING BETWEEEN CONDEMNATION AND CONVICTION

There is no greater basis for a man's confidence than *eternal life.* For one glorious reason, the very term thunders truth of everlasting destiny–security in the heavenlies without end. But eternal life is more than just non-ending life, as blessed a reality as that is! Eternal life is a *quality* of life as well as a *quantity!* That is, there is more than an eternal *sum total* to it, but there's a *surpassing substance* to it. And one of the great confidence-building qualities it provides is the authority that is available to everyone who receives eternal life. The *founding* authority we receive is an authoritative right to affirm, to assert, and proclaim that you *are* a child of God–a son *in* His Son, Jesus Christ! Read it:

> *"But as many as received Him, to them He gave the right to become children of God, to those who believe in His name."* John 1:12

This is an authority conferred upon us by God's will; a position *in Christ* and a pronouncement, "We *are* God's sons!" It's to be walked in and to be lived in *with confidence and certainty* at all times by every believer in Jesus.

But unfortunately, we don't always feel that way. Real sin and personal failure have a way of dimming the brightness. So we need an answer for dealing with the darkness that gathers when we actually *have* sinned and need forgiveness.

Dealing with Sin

1 John 1:7 is an incredibly lovely verse. It makes a moving promise of *ongoing power* through the blood of Jesus Christ when we walk in His light and abide in the fellowship of God's people.

> *"But if we walk in the light as He is in the light, we have fellowship with one another, and the blood of Jesus Christ His Son cleanses us from all sin."* 1 John 1:7

In this verse the Greek text literally emphasizes how the blood of Jesus *keeps on cleansing us* from all sin; how an ongoing, continuous purging process is sustained. That's the environment I invite you to begin and live in, as we walk in the light of Christ's love, His Word, and in the circle of loving, supportive fellowship. But the essential role we have in making this promise work is being wise to deal with sin when it touches, taints, or tarnishes our life with Christ. When the Lord *convicts* us–that is, *points out failure*–we need to respond. But in order to respond *rightly* we need to differentiate between conviction (God's dealing with us about sin) and condemnation (our laboring under guilt without resolving it).

The Difference Between Condemnation and Conviction

Dear brother, it's important that we understand that for us to gain continuous triumph over condemnation, you and I need to recognize this one fact: *condemnation does have grounds to assault us.* Because we do in fact sin, we have sinned, and we are sinners–because of this, we are ever and always vulnerable to being defeated by condemnation. With this fact, because the Holy Spirit faithfully deals with the heart of each humble, honest believer in Jesus, we will regularly sense His conviction when we sin. When He is grieved, we'll know it (Eph. 4:30). However, since our human inclination to condemnation often *feels nearly the same* as conviction does in our soul, we need to gain discernment. So let me make an important distinction between these two biblical terms: conviction and condemnation.

God *does* convict us of sin, but *conviction* is different from *condemnation*. We never need mistake one for the other

30

again–ever.

You ask, "How, Jack? How can I know the difference?"

The answer is clear and unmistakable, for a lifetime of walking with Jesus and in the Word of God has taught me this simple, distinguishing fact: Condemnation *defeats*, but conviction *draws*. Let me elaborate.

Condemnation will always seek to separate you from God. You'll feel driven away by hopelessness and shame. You'll feel unworthy; feel you can't approach Him, and that there's no way in. You'll feel unaccepted–a helpless reject. But there's a holy contrast with conviction.

Conviction will always summon you to God. Conviction beckons you to come to Him, and to say, "I've sinned, but my Savior is waiting to wash me from it all." You'll hear the heart of God's love beating with mercy and promised forgiveness.

No, Sir, the Lord doesn't convict us to punish us, but to get us to repent so His forgiveness can be lavished on us! And the same Holy Spirit that convicts us of sin also convinces us of the adequacy of the righteousness given us in Jesus; He also loves to remind us of the fact that Satan is a beaten adversary, and that we are free to come to the Savior!

This past week, even while working on this message, I had a disappointing experience of failing–of stumbling into an instance of sin. I'm sorry it's not my only sin of recent date, but let me illustrate how we all seem to stumble as I humbly acknowledge my own failure. Just as *you* are determined not to sin, yet sin still subtly finds ways and means to gain a place in your imperfect soul at times, *I too* am committed to living right before God. However, this past week was one of those occasions when I let something slip. It happened like this.

I was involved in a time of recreation with a friend, and during the course of the afternoon at one point I made a remark that was essentially true in content–that is, *technically* true, but it wasn't *completely* so.

I had no sooner said it than I realized I had "hedged," and that there was actually more factual information related to the statement; facts which would qualify the "truth" I had framed in a way so as to be more advantageous to me by leaving the rest of the truth unspoken.

I hadn't really set out to deceive my friend; I really *wasn't* calculating to lie or tell a half-truth. But I did honestly "slip"–slipped into my dilemma, and sud-

...ty that gave
...nt I made.
...mphasized
...hance my
...e how the
...ced and
...g on my
...nce my

...k You
...thful-
...ge it.
...that
...wn

...minut...
...in an
...versation,
...—it would s...
...my earlier "slip,
...o skip it. I laid asid...
...o clarify my words and
...it.

...ng, at home after I had
...and had gone up to my
...t down to write, the whole
...ed across my mind. It wasn't
...gaged in some sort of introspec-
..., raking my soul to find out if I'd
...d that day. In fact, by then, I wasn't
...scious of having done anything that
...ased the Lord. Until . . . until sud-
...y the impression came clearly to my
...d: "Your statement today to (my friend's
...ame) wasn't entirely right."

Now *if* I had plotted or planned to tell a
half-truth, I would have been feeling guilty
the whole rest of the afternoon. But I hadn't.
So when this thought came to me, rather
than bypass it neglectfully *or* endure
condemnation's slow grind, I did two
things—immediately.

First I said, "Lord, You've shown me the

n my personal
sloppy stateme
d me see the way I
f the truth so as to e
earance. In doing so, I s
ot only became unbala
ed, but I see how I was relyi
agement' of the truth to enh
pearance and advance myself."

I continued in prayer: "Lord, I as
to forgive me for both: the slip of tru
ness, and the slowness to acknowled
And also Lord, please strengthen me at
point of weakness which You've just sh
me in my own character."

I haven't related the actual content of m
verbal compromise, because I fear that i
fact too many would think it too small t
deem worthy of my concern. If I were to tell
you what my statement had been, you'd
possibly—indeed, likely—say, "But Pastor
Jack, that wasn't that big a deal!" But you
see, brother, the Holy Spirit *did* deal with
me about it, and that makes anything a *big*
deal! And I've learned that if I keep sensitive to His convicting me about seemingly
"small deals," I'll become protected all the
more against falling carelessly or "slipping"
into *big* failures. The Lord doesn't want to
badger us, but He does want to keep our
conscience sensitive. And confession of sin
when the Spirit points out what *He* thinks
is important is always a wise course. Don't

rationalize conviction of sin. Confes

I did.

And then, after prayer, I did a seco thing. I called my friend.

When he answered the phone, I said, "You know, I really feel dumb calling, but this will only take a minute." I hurried ahead.

"You remember this afternoon when I said (and I described the instance)?" He said he did.

"Well," I went on, "there is another added fact that casts what I said in a different light, and I need to fill out all the pieces."

I continued, explaining, "I didn't mean to intentionally mislead you, but after I'd slipped into a half-truth, the Lord profoundly dealt with me about it–this evening, after I got home." I proceeded to tell him the added information, and when he heard the whole story, he chuckled. "Jack, that's really okay. I understand and accept your feeling the need to tell me. But really, like I said–It's OK."

The truth of the matter is, it would have made no difference at all to my friend. But hear me, brother. *It made a difference to the Lord.* And that made it make a difference to me!

, the most obvious point in my tell-
is is to illustrate how the Spirit's voice
icts; to help urge dealing with
-when-I-see-it-as-sin," rather than
ughing off conviction, rationalizing, or
eing indifferent about it. But here's a
deeper point.

If I were to have only said, "Lord, I
confess my sin," and then claimed, "Praise
God, I'm under His grace and all my sins
are forgiven!" I'd have left something else
half done. I would have failed to move on
to the decisive actions required for "walking in the light"; that is, exposing what was
hidden, and taking steps to ensure unbro-
ken integrity in my fellowship with a brother
as well as with God. To fail to follow through
at the second point would be to end by
backing out on the key issue spiritual
maturity requires: keeping my relationships uncluttered–with both God *and* man!

To "walk in light" means to confront sin.
Because sin *is* a factor in all our lives,
confronting it is important. But we need to
learn to do that in an atmosphere that's
without condemnation! Conviction is *not*
something God wields like a sword over our
necks, lovelessly slicing His critiques at us.
He's not in the business of dealing in a
heavy-handed, condemning manner.
Rather, to the contrary, in His infinite
mercy, gentleness and graciousness, God
is constantly reaching out to assist us in

the process of being freed from sin in all its most sinister or most subtle ways. That's His business as our Redeemer, Incredible Lover, and Savior from sin, marvelous in patience and lovingkindness, with a mercy beyond our ability to find out.

But He does bring us to confrontation with sin.

> *"If we say that we have fellowship with Him, and walk in darkness, we lie and do not practice the truth. If we say that we have no sin, we deceive ourselves, and the truth is not in us. If we say that we have not sinned, we make Him a liar, and His word is not in us."*
> *1 John 1:6, 8, 10.*

Those three verses focus a demanding point. They say that if I'm having fellowship with God, and yet I insistently, intentionally, and by my own will walk in the darkness of self-justification or indifference to sin, then I'm not walking in the truth. And there's no way in the world I'm going to escape feeling condemned if I'm in willful pursuit of that which is contrary to the way of the Lord!

Hey, listen! I'm not talking about accidental failures, fumblings, or evidences of your human weakness. That's another issue, even though those matters–like my own slip I described–are in a different league from what these verses of scripture are addressing. They point up the danger of not coming to terms with any willful pursuit of sin–my own will, my own way, my own sin. If these are unrepented of when you're *convicted*, you *will* bring inevitable feelings of condemnation upon yourself, and that condemnation is inescapable apart from repentance. This book's message and the promised hope it holds do not apply unless a no-slack-for-sin mindset governs our commitment. I may sin, but I won't excuse it, I'll confess it.

The above verses remind us that sin needs to be confronted–to be dealt with *regularly*. They aren't to drum sin's guilt into our system, but to trumpet truthfulness into our ears. Their point isn't to negate the beautiful things God says about our forgiveness in Christ. No! The point is to show me that I'm living a dumb-fool, ostrich-kind- of-life if I stick my head in the sand of supposed "grace" and say, "Hey, man, know what? I just don't have a sin problem. Not me, brother! Nada."

But we *do*. We all do. I do, you do, etc. And that's not a matter of issuing a license for more sin, by excusing myself with a glib, "Don't expect me to be perfect" as a pious excuse for lolling in self-indulgence.

So the bottom line is: There's no way to be freed from condemnation without first confronting the reality of sin. Whether I'm a person who has walked in the sanctifying grace of Jesus Christ for most of my lifetime or a newborn babe who just received Jesus this week, the same need is present. We need to recognize that you and I are people with whom the sin problem is very real, both around us and in us. Indeed, there are fragments of it in our flesh. They're fragments that we'll never be wormed free of until Jesus gives us another body at His coming, and so, we need to face the reality of sin, but we need to face it both wisely and honestly. Wisdom will keep us in the light of the Word, and in the fullness of that light of truth, two things will happen: (1) We'll be kept free from condemnation, and (2) we'll keep honest in dealing with sin.

Conviction will always point out sin, but only to drive us to deal with it, not drill us with guilt. Condemnation doesn't stand a chance when conviction is responded to with confession. Because confession, in the light of the power-cluster of confidence-building verses we're about to study, will neutralize the crippling effects of condemnation:

• Your assurance before God will be secured;

• Your confidence in life will rise with joy; and

• Your fruitfulness in ministry will be

certain, continual, and abundant.

It's all possible through the power of God's words of truth from His Word of Truth!

TALK ABOUT IT!   Chapter questions to explore with a friend.

1.   What is the chief difference between conviction and condemnation?

2.   What are two things of which the Holy Spirit convicts us ongoingly?

3.   There is no way of being free from condemnation without *first* confronting the reality of _____.

CHAPTER FOUR:

THE POWER-CLUSTER VE.

The stories of believers who succum
a less-than confident experience are p.
fully too common. For example, I recall
story of a person I'll refer to as Glen.
wrote to me about how he had carried
sense of guilt and condemnation for 2
years of his life. Almost all of those years, h
had known Jesus Christ as his Savior
having a genuine confidence he was
born-again. But still, he never could completely shake the gnawing sense of guilt that
related to past episodes in his life. His letter
referred to a transforming Sunday—one day
when I related a message centered on a
power-cluster of verses; a set of scriptures
which had a tremendous life-changing impact on him. By his own testimony, that
power-cluster "broke the bondage" to condemnation! The truth of God's Word set him
free and changed his life as the condemning
spirit which had so tormented him for two
decades was crushed!

Those same verses, which brought such
a resounding victory in this one person's
life, have done the same for many who have

estified of the same release. This power-cluster constitutes the verses I want to study with you now. But here are a half dozen verses which can provide effective weaponry for keeping the taunts of condemnation at bay when they attack you, and assuring your being equipped against this vicious, lying enemy of our souls.

First, let me list the six verses from God's Word which I have been referring to as "the power-cluster" verses. I've called them that because they remind me of the air-warfare tactic of "cluster-bombing." This has been a means employed for decades of battle, insuring that a target is totally obliterated—that the enemy has no remaining point of retaliation. In the same way, my objective is to see your heart and mind grip the reality in these texts of scripture in a way that will make them your weapons against the Enemy. Thus, *every* time he seeks to deceive you with condemnation, you can obliterate him with these tactical weapons of God's eternal, unchanging truth.

The six verses which have found "cluster-power" in my own experience are: 1 John 1:9; Romans 8:1; Isaiah 1:18, 44:22; Micah 7:18, 19; Psalm 103:11, 12; and Hebrews 10:17. They are equally divided into two sets of three: the *root* of reality, and the *fruit* of rejoicing. Let me outline them briefly, then elaborate.

I. THE ROOT OF REALITY

A. 1 John 1:9 - The reality of God's readiness to forgive.

B. Romans 8:1 - The reality of God's justice in forgiving.

C. Isaiah 1:18; 44:22 - The reality of God's totality in forgiveness.

II. THE FRUIT OF REJOICING

A. Micah 7:18, 19 - Rejoicing in overwhelming mercy.

B. Psalm 103:11, 12 - Rejoicing in an undiscoverable record.

C. Hebrews 10:17 - Rejoicing in an unreclaimable past.

God's Readiness To Forgive

"If we confess our sins, He is faithful and just to forgive us our sins and to cleanse us from all unrighteousness." 1 John 1:9

This was the verse that the Holy Spirit breathed into my soul that night as I sat in despair on the brick casement in the center of my college campus that moonlit night. Here's a dual concept about God's nature that we need to see.

First, see God's readiness and reliability to forgive: "He is *faithful* to forgive us, and to cleanse us from ALL (get it, *ALL*!!) unrigh-teousness." Perhaps nothing moved me more than the sudden revelation that God wanted to show me *His* faithfulness not-withstanding my *un*-faithfulness. I was amazed at the immediate sense I felt of this grand fact: God is incapable of unforgiveness! If the simple condition of confession is met, He cannot, He will not, He is unable to deny His commitment to be a Forgiver!!

Further, this forgiveness is not delayed to see how you or I will do another day. It is present-tense, on-the-spot, here-and-now forgiveness! And that sets up the second feature of the matter: He performs His forgiveness as totally as He does quickly: ". . . to cleanse us from ALL!"

Oh, how my heart leaps at that word! And may yours as well, dear brother. God is not operating an installment plan in forgiving us, as though increments of guilt were "washed away" on the basis of our performance over a season of days, weeks, or months. Get it! ALL is forgiven–And right NOW!

God's Justice In Forgiveness

"There is therefore now no con-demnation to them who are in Christ Jesus." Romans 8:1

Our first verse included a significant

phrase: "He is . . . just" as well as forgiving. This verse in Romans brings us face to face with that gigantic truth.

When the Bible says that IN CHRIST there is NO CONDEMNATION, we are being told that, literally, " There is no more judgment of the court being brought down upon or against us any more." Such words remind us of a fact we must never forget: Heaven's laws cannot be broken without a price being paid. In other words, God *must* remain just at the same time He is loving.

The fact of your sin and mine is that it cannot simply be forgiven "out of hand," so to speak. Forgiveness must have *grounds*; that is, the problem of sin's penalty cannot be dispensed with as though a clerk tore up the price tag on a suit and gave it to you free. Even if you receive it without cost, somebody has to pay for it.

So it is with the clothing of God's righteousness–the highest-priced suit ever worn by a man. That garment of perfectly tailored salvation and forgiveness which the Father gives us when we put our faith in Jesus Christ is only available because Jesus paid for it with His life-blood. And the reason that payment was so worthy was because of His perfect sinlessness.

Thus it is that the *grounds* of our forgiveness have been established in that God's justice–His inviolable laws which require payment for sin–was completely satisfied. The life of His sinless Son was exchanged to balance the scales of justice which required payment for *my* sin, for *your* sin–for *all* sin.

There was a popular song years ago, and you'll still hear it sung occasionally: "Though it makes Him sad to see the way we live, He'll always say, 'I forgive.' " That song is true, but in a distorted way; a half-truth worse than an entire *un*truth. By featuring His forgiveness *alone*, God's love is paraded, without accountability for God's justice; God's forgiveness apart from the price of Jesus' Cross. He does say, *and always will*–"I forgive." But He also says that forgiveness comes solely through His Son.

Further, because God says Jesus satisfied the demands of heaven's justice, in effect God says, "In forgiving you, I will attribute to you my Son's record of sinlessness and at the same time abolish your own personal record of sin and sinning!" The impact of such a concept is staggering to *anyone* who truly wraps his mind and heart around it. No analogy can come close to being a faithful representation of this amazing reality, but here's a simple picture to help us.

Say, you have a Gold MasterCard, Visa, American Express, or some such credit tool. And you have this Gold Card because you've run up $66 trillion of indebtedness. Now, the obvious stares at you: there's simply no way you can ever pay it. However, there is a fellow cardholder, named Jesus, who offers to put your debt on His card. His account is debt free, and His resource is capable of "handling" any amount transferred. But as though that weren't enough, He *now* takes on your card's obligations. In essence, you switch account numbers; switch identities. So the Bank will now come *after Him* instead of you, as they seek payment on the debt.

And brother, that's what happened! The price was death, and death *did* come after Jesus as He went to the Cross to make the full and final payment for our indebtedness-our sin. And at that point, as He died on the Cross, for judgment's and condemnation's purposes–for satisfying justice's demands–He was *you* and He was *me*. In a way transcending imagination He bore all of us and our sin on the Cross, becoming the ultimate payment for the penalty of our sin.

So the debt was paid. Our account balance before God is zero. We owe no penalties to God's justice for our sins. Payment's been made.

We are justified, and now no judgment can be "brought down against"–no condemnation. The Judge–the Living God–has made a statement in the courtroom of heaven as the Judge of the universe. The gavel has sounded and He has said, "I declare all of those who have received My Son as Savior as having the same degree of guiltlessness that He has." And He is *just* in doing that, as well as loving and forgiving, by reason of the fact that Jesus Himself bore all sin, paid sin's price, and rose again to prove it was all true. It was impossible that death hold Him, because our sin which He bore could find no control over Him. And in rising from the dead, He now comes as Heaven's attorney, declaring: "The Judge's case is dismissed. You've been pronounced 'Not guilty,' and totally accepted in the sight of the Judge of the heavens–Almighty God." You're justified–acquitted of any record of sin against you! 'There *is* therefore no condemnation'–no case whatsoever against you in the chambers of divine justice!" Hallelujah! Shout it again–HALLELUJAH!

Now that's true, and our praise is proper. There *is* no "case held against me," that is, no judgment "coming down on my head." But that doesn't mean there isn't an occasional battle over this decision heaven's court has declared.

Dealing with the Enemy's Torment

Someone says, "Right! If there is 'Now no condemnation,' why do I feel it sometimes?" The answer involves two related reasons.

First, as human beings, our memories

often haunt us, conjuring the past like a recurring nightmare or an endless video-tape rehearsing one failure after another. Second, we are still vulnerable to the Adversary's ploys. A relentless Adversary, the devil tirelessly comes as a prosecutor, accusing us as a lying Lawyer from hell. He *does* have a case, in *half*-truth. He is taunting us for real sins, but he wants to press his charges without reference to what Jesus has done for us and what we have received in Him.

Picture a courtroom.

Bill, a believer in Christ, has just failed. Anxiously, gleefully, the Lawyer-from-hell runs into the Courtroom of the Universe and slams down a report of the crime: "Bill sinned!" This hellish attorney is seething; driven by a perverted mixture of loathing and delight: "Bill's dead this time!" And claiming Bill's failure justifies his argument, the devil presents his case against Bill before God, our Father and Judge.

But Bill has earlier conferred with his Heavenly Attorney, Jesus, whom he met earlier before the adversary's present court date. Bill had already put the case of his whole life *totally* into the hands of Jesus, via his confession of sin. So when the Judge asks the Defense to come forward, our Heavenly Attorney presents the blood of His Cross and His sinless life as grounds for the

Judge to refuse to accept the Liar's true charges. Jesus says, "Yes, Bill sinned. But I hold up the evidence of what has been accomplished on My Cross." And brother, when He does that, that blood is still as crimson and fresh in power as the day it poured forth from our Heavenly Attorney's own veins! So it is that our Father, the just Judge, looks at the two cases—one *against* Bill and one *for* him, and He says, "I've studied the evidence, and I find the defendant 'not guilty!' The evidence of the Blood is greater than the evidence of Bill's failure!"

The Lawyer-from-hell shoots out of his chair screaming, "On what grounds, Your Eminence? This man broke YOUR law!!"

And the Father narrows His gaze, His eyes burning with righteousness, and addressing Satan, the prosecuting attorney, He points His finger at His Son, whose scars and blood still speak in heaven, and says, *"On the grounds of the payment you see standing before you.* Case dismissed!" And the thunder of His gavel drives the prosecuting lawyer from the room.

Racing down the halls in fury, the Lawyer-from-hell vows to himself to find another child of God who perhaps does not have the same degree of understanding that Bill had; someone who will not so immediately and thoroughly confer with the Heavenly Attorney, so that the case may be decided so quickly and so completely. The Lawyer-from-hell knows he can't easily separate such a child of God from His inheritance of eternal life, but he'll still seek to plague him through distortions of the written Word; he'll attempt to wreak an agony of mental and emotional litigation for weeks–maybe years, if he finds a child of God who is ignorant of the great truth: "NO CONDEMNATION!"

God's Totality of Forgiveness

" 'Come now, and let us reason together,' says the Lord, 'Though your sins are like scarlet, they shall be as white as snow; though they are red like crimson, they shall be as wool.' " Isaiah 1:18

There's nearly a holy touch of humor in this verse.

I don't know why it is that I picture this at the table on the patio of Anna's and my house, but I do. It is as though I see God saying, "Come here, Jack. I want to talk with you–We're going to 'reason together.' "

That's where the humor begins; I mean, who is capable of "reasoning" with Ultimate Intelligence, with the Mastermind of the Universe? But God still says, "I want you to think this through–let us reason together."

Then, having said that, He adds words that from our human point of view are absolutely *un*-reasonable. He adds:

"Everything that has indelibly stained your record is going to be expunged. There is no failure so severe, no sin so destructive, no guilt so deep, no action so depraved, corrupt, or damaging, that it can survive the penetrating power of the cleansing agent I am using."

Listen to His reasoning. He is basing His "reason" *on His terms*–Christ's Cross–not on ours. Our "reasoning" will end up arguing that it's all too gracious and all so undeserved. Our minds will plead guilty upon remembrance of our failures, and the residue of our past will stare us in the face and scream that we're fakes who are pretending a piety we don't possess. But God keeps saying, *"Come on now! Reason with Me,"* which is His way of saying, "I want you to think like I do." That dimension of "thought" is described elsewhere in this same prophecy of Isaiah's. God is speaking, and says:

> *"For as the heavens are higher than the earth, so are My ways higher than your ways, and My thoughts than your thoughts."*
> *Isaiah 55:9*

God's appeal to us is that we *not* appeal to our *own* reasoning, but to HIS! He isn't unreasonable in declaring such forgiveness, because the reason for it all is JESUS! And it is from the roots of these truths that we are called to taste, eat, and delight in the fruit of rejoicing!

TALK ABOUT IT! Chapter questions to explore with a friend.

1.   There's a dual concept about God's nature reflected in 1 John 1:9, "He is faithful and just to forgive us our sins. . ." How do these two facets of God's nature relate to you personally?

2.   How would you describe the doctrinal concept of "justification"?

3.   In what ways is Satan like a "Lawyer-from-hell"? On what grounds is a child of God able to withstand the accusations of the Lawyer-from-hell?

CHAPTER FIVE:

MASTERING GUILT
AND CONDEMNATION

Isaiah was a man like you. He was conscious of his limitations at a time that God was calling him to become an instrument in His hands. Listen to him:

"Oh, God–It's awful. I don't have anything together! My mouth betrays me, I don't talk like a man whom You'd call Yours; in fact, my lips seem fouled by the things I've said. And worse, Lord, everything around me is like that. How can I become a whole man, much less a holy one, when everything around me smacks of human sin and hellish trash?"

You say, "Did a prophet say that?" And Isaiah did. You can read it in Isaiah 6:5, and the setting is significant. It was right at the time the Lord was seeking to show this one man that He had higher purposes for him than he had ever imagined. Could it be that's exactly where God is in dealing with you?

My paraphrase above is not exaggerated in the least. What Isaiah experienced of a *sense of disqualification* is so common to us men, maybe we'd be wise to all make one of our middle names "Isaiah" as a reminder.

But in making that reminder, we would end with a positive power, for Isaiah's sense of condemnation was smashed by God's cleansing power: "Look ... Your iniquity is taken away and your sin is purged!" (Isaiah 6:6).

And that, Sir, is the purpose of this book, to bring you to a place of *ministry readiness*; not as a religious professional, but as God's-man-on-*your*-job! It begins with knowing the *root* system in the power-cluster, but it climaxes with knowing the song of rejoicing which flows from the *fruit* of the power-cluster.

It's a holy wine. And it makes you sing, like Isaiah was ignited to sing: "Sing ... for the Lord has done it!"

Done what? Listen, here's what!

> *"I have blotted out, like a thick*
> *cloud, your transgressions, and like*
> *a cloud, your sins. Return to Me,*
> *for I have redeemed you!"*
> *Isaiah 44:22*

Isaiah's discovery is one that invites your and my sharing. Hear the truth that *shouts* the dimensions of our forgiveness. To measure the scope of this salvation is to find its measurelessness, but in hearing the thunder of heaven's announcement about my sin's banishment and my total acceptance, I can't help but sing.

Sir, I ask you to prepare to lift your voice in song. But only after you've taken a drink from the wine born of the power-cluster of the grapes of God's graciousness. Read, then sing:

Rejoicing in Overwhelming Mercy

"Who is a God like You, pardoning iniquity and passing over the transgression of the remnant of His heritage? He does not retain His anger forever, because He delights in mercy. He will again have compassion on us, and will subdue our iniquities. You will cast all our sins into the depths of the sea." Micah 7:18-19

Hear that!? Sins *buried* in the depths of the sea! Are you aware that the deepest point in the oceans of this world are further down than the highest point of the mountains on earth? The message: There's nothing I've "run up" as a debt of sin, that the sea of God's forgiveness can't cover–and bury! Sing!

"O the deep, deep love of Jesus,
Vast unmeasured boundless, free!
Rolling as a mighty ocean

56

active, committed Redeer
will to forget those sins.'
us that the very thing y
be a *power* if *we* wer
power He possesses.
that He does have the
sin, but that He has and w
selectively removed from our r
sinful facts of our lives!

Some time ago I was touched by what
brother shared with me. After having failed
at a point of sin often besetting him, he had
prayed, saying, "Lord, I don't even feel I
deserve to come to You today about this...
I've failed this way so many times. I'm here
today because I did it again." Then, he said,
"The Holy Spirit whispered the words of the
Father to me, and said, '*Did what again?*'"

"*Did what* again?" Can you hear it? It
was only in *that* moment that my friend said
[..]e truly understood how fully Father God
[..]eans, "Their sins I will remember no
[..]ore." After we have confessed our sins,
[..]t only have they been removed com-
[..]etely from the books of heaven, but by His
[..]wer God has chosen to remove them
[..]ever from His mind!

[..]hy? Only because of the Cross of our
[..]d Jesus Christ.

[..]was also profoundly impressed by a
[..]y someone shared with me after a mes-
[..]I brought from this text: "I will *remem-*

In its fullness over me."

Samuel Francis

*"Buried in the deepest sea,
Yes, that's good enough for me.
I shall live eternally,
Praise God, my sins are gone!"*

Helen Griggs

Rejoicing In Your Undiscoverable Record

"For as the heavens are high above the earth, so great is His mercy toward those who fear Him; as far as the east is from the west, so far has He removed our transgressions from us." Psalm 103:11, 12

There is a studied effort on God's part to make a picture so clear in our earth-bound minds that we can't forget it. "As far as the east is from the west" is a tangible figure any thoughtful mind can grasp. If God had said, "as far as the north from south," the distance would be impressive, but not immeasurable. It is approximately 12,500 miles from the North Pole to the South Pole. Once that trip is traversed, the very next instant–from any point south–a new direction is established: *back to the north.* And unfortunately, that's what many people do with their sin. They take it to one end of God's promise of forgiveness, then carry the load "back north" again, making wearying cycles of repeated conjurings up of memories of failure. But God's Word won't allow that, not with the clear image He's engraved on its pages: *"As far as east from west."* Get it straight once and for all: that's *eternally apart, permanently removed, gone forever.*

One never comes to the end of that distance. It's as though God put a rocket into orbit, with the payload made up of our sins. Then, having orbited the earth–whirling to the east from the west–it gained escape velocity and now has been launched into the infinite, black void of space, plummeting into the depths of the universe. Brother, it will never return; our forgiven sins will never find re-entry. Sing!

> *"Amazing grace, how sweet the sound,*
> *That saved a wretch like me.*
> *I once was lost but now am found,*
> *Was blind but now I see!"*

John Newton

"Cleansing power, in this hour
Wash my heart and all sin erase.
Blood of Jesus, flow and free us,
Lead us Lord to Your resting place."

JWH

...icing In An Unreclaimable Past

...aps the master stroke of all texts in ...ower-cluster is found in these mighty ...s which occur three times in the Bible, ... though God wanted to establish a ...hree-fold witness" to this rich reality: ...Heaven FORGETS the record of our past!

> *"Their sins and their lawless deeds I will remember no more."*
> Hebrews 10:17 *

How can this be? How can the greates... mind in the universe "forget"? Isn't forge... fulness a sign of mental weakness? We... consider this.

If you or I could take the most unplea... memory of our lives–the one thing that... comes back in a nightmare; the re... brance of the worst moment we've... experienced; if we could selectivel... such ugliness from our memories... wouldn't we consider that capabilit... power?

Of course we would!

So, listen: God is saying He... power! He isn't saying He can't... our sins anymore. We're not de... senile parent who's losing a... memory. Rather, this text tea...

*(see also Jer. 31:34; Isa.43:...

ber their sins *no more!*" They said: "Pastor Hayford, as you spoke of God forgetting our sins, though I believed what you were saying, I had difficulty understanding how it could be. Then the Lord brought to mind something that happened where I work.

"I work about 30-35 miles north of here," the person continued, "and just last week a thunder storm struck, and a lightning bolt hit the transformer on the power line behind our office where I work. Because it didn't actually destroy anything visible, at first we took little notice. But later we discovered that when that bolt struck the transformer, a power surge coursed through our computer systems and everything that had been input for that day had been totally and irrevocably erased!

"When I stepped to the office door and looked out where the lightning struck, the telephone pole appeared to me as though it were a giant cross, with the burned out transformer just hanging there on the pole. And as you spoke tonight, it struck me: Jesus was the one who, hanging on the Cross, transformed us from death unto life by totally absorbing the lightning bolt of divine judgment for our sin. Just as He bore the payment of death for my sin, He also occasioned a power surge of God's might which went shooting into heaven's records of our sins and totally erased all the memory banks!"

My eyes misted. But my heart sang as I heard this analogy. And I bid you, brother–go forth as a *Man Alive* in Christ! Go forward singing!

> *"And can it be that I should gain*
> *an int'rest in the Savior's blood?*
> *. . . Long my imprisoned spirit lay*
> *Fast bound in sin and nature's night*
> *Thine eye diffused a quick'ning ray,*
> *I woke, the dungeon flamed with light!*
> *My chains fell off, my heart was free,*
> *I rose, went forth and followed Thee."*

Charles Wesley

The Grapes of Grace

The fruit of rejoicing which comprises the power-cluster of anti-condemnation verses are the Grapes of Grace–not wrath; and they blend together to make a holy wine, not a heady one. Think about it, Sir.

Have you ever noticed how bold some people become when they drink? How happy (even if only temporarily)? How open and tender?

All those traits distill from the wine of earthly vineyards, but in this cluster of fruit-filled verses we're looking at, there is genuine *confidence* for any man.

- Confidence that brings a boldness in your stance before God.

In its fullness over me."

Samuel Francis

"Buried in the deepest sea,
Yes, that's good enough for me.
I shall live eternally,
Praise God, my sins are gone!"

Helen Griggs

Rejoicing In Your Undiscoverable Record

"For as the heavens are high above
the earth, so great is His mercy
toward those who fear Him; as far
as the east is from the west, so far
has He removed our transgressions
from us."   Psalm 103:11, 12

There is a studied effort on God's part to make a picture so clear in our earth-bound minds that we can't forget it. "As far as the east is from the west" is a tangible figure any thoughtful mind can grasp. If God had said, "as far as the north from south," the distance would be impressive, but not immeasurable. It is approximately 12,500 miles from the North Pole to the South Pole. Once that trip is traversed, the very next instant–from any point south–a new direction is established: *back to the north.* And unfortunately, that's what many people do with their sin. They take it to one end of God's promise of forgiveness, then carry the

57

load "back north" again, making wearying cycles of repeated conjurings up of memories of failure. But God's Word won't allow that, not with the clear image He's engraved on its pages: *"As far as east from west."* Get it straight once and for all: that's *eternally apart, permanently removed, gone forever.*

One never comes to the end of that distance. It's as though God put a rocket into orbit, with the payload made up of our sins. Then, having orbited the earth–whirling to the east from the west–it gained escape velocity and now has been launched into the infinite, black void of space, plummeting into the depths of the universe. Brother, it will never return; our forgiven sins will never find re-entry. Sing!

> *"Amazing grace, how sweet the sound,*
> *That saved a wretch like me.*
> *I once was lost but now am found,*
> *Was blind but now I see!"*
>
> John Newton
>
> *"Cleansing power, in this hour*
> *Wash my heart and all sin erase.*
> *Blood of Jesus, flow and free us,*
> *Lead us Lord to Your resting place."*
>
> JWH

Perhaps the master stroke of all texts in the power-cluster is found in these mighty words which occur three times in the Bible, as though God wanted to establish a "three-fold witness" to this rich reality: *Heaven FORGETS the record of our past!*

> *"Their sins and their lawless deeds*
> *I will remember no more."*
> *Hebrews 10:17 ***

How can this be? How can the greatest mind in the universe "forget"? Isn't forgetfulness a sign of mental weakness? Well, consider this.

If you or I could take the most unpleasant memory of our lives–the one thing that most comes back in a nightmare; the remembrance of the worst moment we've ever experienced; if we could selectively slice such ugliness from our memories forever, wouldn't we consider that capability a great *power?*

Of course we would!

So, listen: God is saying He has that power! He isn't saying He *can't* remember our sins anymore. We're not dealing with a senile parent who's losing a grip on His memory. Rather, this text teaches us of an

---

*(see also Jer. 31:34; Isa.43:25; Heb. 8:12)

active, committed Redeemer who says, "I *will* to forget those sins." And He's telling us that the very thing you and I feel would be a *power* if *we* were capable of it, is a power He possesses. And He not only says *that He does have the power to forget our sin, but that* He has and *will* do it. He has selectively removed from our record all the sinful facts of our lives!

Some time ago I was touched by what a brother shared with me. After having failed at a point of sin often besetting him, he had prayed, saying, "Lord, I don't even feel I deserve to come to You today about this... I've failed this way so many times. I'm here today because I did it again." Then, he said, "The Holy Spirit whispered the words of the Father to me, and said, *'Did what again?'* "

"Did what again?" Can you hear it? It was only in *that* moment that my friend said he truly understood how fully Father God means, "Their sins I will remember no more." After we have confessed our sins, not only have they been removed completely from the books of heaven, but by His power God has chosen to remove them *forever* from His mind!

Why? Only because of the Cross of our Lord Jesus Christ.

I was also profoundly impressed by a story someone shared with me after a message I brought from this text: "I will *remem-*

And claim the crown
   through Christ my own.
Amazing love!
How can it be
That Thou, my God,
   shouldst die for me!"

Charles Wesley

TALK ABOUT IT! Chapter questions to explore with a friend.

1.   Five specific ways of mastering guilt and condemnation were mentioned in this chapter. Can you cite three of them and discuss how you've experienced success in any one of them recently?

2.   Discuss one of the three dramatic illustrations given in this chapter which demonstrate how God has dealt with our sins.

3.   Why hasn't God removed our sins from us as far as the north is from the south?

Scriptural Ammunition
Against Guilt
and Condemnation

The following pages are four sets of the "power-cluster" verses. They are intended to be removed from this book and to be used for memorization, to keep in your wallet or Bible, and extra sets are included for you to give to other men.

The Power-Cluster Verses

1 John 1:9
The reality of God's readiness to forgive.

"If we confess our sins, He is faithful and just to forgive us our sins and to cleanse us from all unrighteousness."

Romans 8:1
The reality of God's justice in forgiving.

"There is therefore now no condemnation to those who are in Christ Jesus, who do not walk according to the flesh, but according to the Spirit."

Isaiah 1:18; 44:22
The reality of God's totality in forgiveness.

" 'Come now, and let us reason together,' Says the Lord, ' Though your sins are like scarlet, they shall be as white as snow; though they are red like crimson, they shall be as wool.' "

"I have blotted out, like a thick cloud, your transgressions, and like a cloud, your sins. Return to Me, for I have redeemed you."

Micah 7:18, 19
Rejoicing in overwhelming mercy.

"Who is a God like You, pardoning iniquity and passing over the transgression of the remnant of His heritage? He does not retain His anger forever, because He delights in mercy. He will again have compassion on us, and will subdue our iniquities. You will cast all our sins into the depths of the sea."

Psalm 103: 11, 12
Rejoicing in an undiscoverable record.

"For as the heavens are high above the earth, so great is His mercy toward those who fear Him; as far as the east is from the west, so far has He removed our transgressions from us."

Hebrews 10:17
Rejoicing in an unreclaimable past.

"Their sins and their lawless deeds I will remember no more."

The Power-Cluster Verses

1 John 1:9
The reality of God's readiness
to forgive.

"If we confess our sins, He is faithful and just to forgive us our sins and to cleanse us from all unrighteousness."

Romans 8:1
The reality of God's justice
in forgiving.

"There is therefore now no condemnation to those who are in Christ Jesus, who do not walk according to the flesh, but according to the Spirit."

Isaiah 1:18; 44:22
The reality of God's totality
in forgiveness.

" 'Come now, and let us reason together,' Says the Lord, 'Though your sins are like scarlet, they shall be as white as snow; though they are red like crimson, they shall be as wool.' "

"I have blotted out, like a thick cloud, your transgressions, and like a cloud, your sins. Return to Me, for I have redeemed you."

Micah 7:18, 19
Rejoicing in overwhelming mercy.

"Who is a God like You, pardoning iniquity and passing over the transgression of the remnant of His heritage? He does not retain His anger forever, because He delights in mercy. He will again have compassion on us, and will subdue our iniquities. You will cast all our sins into the depths of the sea."

Psalm 103: 11, 12
Rejoicing in an undiscoverable record.

"For as the heavens are high above the earth, so great is His mercy toward those who fear Him; as far as the east is from the west, so far has He removed our transgressions from us."

Hebrews 10:17
Rejoicing in an unreclaimable past.

"Their sins and their lawless deeds I will remember no more."

The Power-Cluster Verses

1 John 1:9
The reality of God's readiness
to forgive.

"If we confess our sins, He is faithful and just to forgive us our sins and to cleanse us from all unrighteousness."

Romans 8:1
The reality of God's justice
in forgiving.

"There is therefore now no condemnation to those who are in Christ Jesus, who do not walk according to the flesh, but according to the Spirit."

Isaiah 1:18; 44:22
The reality of God's totality
in forgiveness.

" 'Come now, and let us reason together,' Says the Lord, ' Though your sins are like scarlet, they shall be as white as snow; though they are red like crimson, they shall be as wool.' "

"I have blotted out, like a thick cloud, your transgressions, and like a cloud, your sins. Return to Me, for I have redeemed you."

Micah 7:18, 19
Rejoicing in overwhelming mercy.

"Who is a God like You, pardoning iniquity and passing over the transgression of the remnant of His heritage? He does not retain His anger forever, because He delights in mercy. He will again have compassion on us, and will subdue our iniquities. You will cast all our sins into the depths of the sea."

Psalm 103: 11, 12
Rejoicing in an undiscoverable record.

"For as the heavens are high above the earth, so great is His mercy toward those who fear Him; as far as the east is from the west, so far has He removed our transgressions from us."

Hebrews 10:17
Rejoicing in an unreclaimable past.

"Their sins and their lawless deeds I will remember no more."

The Power-Cluster Verses

1 John 1:9
The reality of God's readiness
to forgive.

"If we confess our sins, He is faithful and just to forgive us our sins and to cleanse us from all unrighteousness."

Romans 8:1
The reality of God's justice
in forgiving.

"There is therefore now no condemnation to those who are in Christ Jesus, who do not walk according to the flesh, but according to the Spirit."

Isaiah 1:18; 44:22
The reality of God's totality
in forgiveness.

" 'Come now, and let us reason together,' Says the Lord, 'Though your sins are like scarlet, they shall be as white as snow; though they are red like crimson, they shall be as wool.' "

"I have blotted out, like a thick cloud, your transgressions, and like a cloud, your sins. Return to Me, for I have redeemed you."

Micah 7:18, 19
Rejoicing in overwhelming mercy.

"Who is a God like You, pardoning iniquity and passing over the transgression of the remnant of His heritage? He does not retain His anger forever, because He delights in mercy. He will again have compassion on us, and will subdue our iniquities. You will cast all our sins into the depths of the sea."

Psalm 103: 11, 12
Rejoicing in an undiscoverable record.

"For as the heavens are high above the earth, so great is His mercy toward those who fear Him; as far as the east is from the west, so far has He removed our transgressions from us."

Hebrews 10:17
Rejoicing in an unreclaimable past.

"Their sins and their lawless deeds I will remember no more."

Receiving Christ As Lord and Savior

It seems possible that some earnest inquirer may have read this book and somehow still never have received Jesus Christ as his personal Savior. If that's true of you, that you have never personally welcomed the Lord Jesus into your heart, to be your Savior and to lead you in the matters of your life, I would like to encourage and help you to do that.

There is no need to delay, for an honest heart can approach the loving Father God at any time. So I'd like to invite you to come with me and let's pray to Him right now.

If it's possible there where you are, bow your head—or even kneel, if you can. But in either case, let me pray a simple prayer first—then, I've added words for you to pray yourself:

My Prayer:

"Father God, I have the privilege of joining with this child of Yours who is reading this book right now. I want to thank You for the openness of heart being shown toward You, and I want to praise You for Your promise, that when we call to You, You will answer.

"I know that genuine sincerity is present in this heart, which is ready to speak this prayer, and so we come to You in the Name and through the Cross of Your Son, the Lord

Jesus. Thank You for hearing." (And now, you speak your prayer.)

Your Prayer:

"Dear God, I am doing this because I believe in Your love for me, and I want to ask You to come to me as I come to You. Please help me now.

"First, I thank You for sending Your Son Jesus to earth to live and to die for me on the Cross. I thank You for the gift of forgiveness of sin that You offer me now, and I pray for that forgiveness.

"Do, I pray, forgive me and cleanse my life in Your sight, through the blood of Jesus Christ. I am sorry for anything and everything I have ever done that is unworthy in Your sight. Please take away all guilt and condemnation, as I accept the fact that Jesus died to pay for all my sins, and through Him I am now given forgiveness on this earth and eternal life in heaven.

"I ask You, Lord Jesus, please come into my life now. Because You rose from the dead, I know You're alive and I want You to live with me—now and forever.

"I am turning my life over to You, and turning from my way to Yours. I invite Your Holy Spirit to fill me and lead me forward in a life that will please the Heavenly Father.

"Thank You for hearing me. From this

day forward, I commit myself to Jesus Christ the Son of God. In His Name, Amen."

DEVOTIONS

IN THE FIRST EIGHT CHAPTERS OF

ROMANS

Contributed by Bob Anderson

The Book of Romans is widely regarded as the greatest exposition of Christian doctrine in the entire Bible. The plan of redemption is developed throughout the whole epistle, building with clear logic, graced with holy passion.

The song writer's words, "Our hope is built on nothing less than Jesus' blood and righteousness," reminds us of Romans set to music. The grounds for our confidence truly is on Christ the Solid Rock–and no exposition has ever presented a stronger, more exhaustive legal case for that confidence than Romans.

(It is suggested that this devotional be used for stimulating discussion and prayer within a small group of men meeting regularly.)

☐ **Today's Text: Romans 1:1-7** *(key v. 4)*

1 **Today's Truth:** Jesus' Sonship was actually "declared" or reaffirmed by His Resurrection. Because we, as believers, are "in Him" as sons, therefore our sonship is assured beyond any doubt because *His resurrection guarantees it.*

Today's Thoughts: _____

_____

_____

☐ **Today's Text: Romans 1:8-15** *(key v.12)*

2 **Today's Truth:** Even the Apostle Paul, being the "powerhouse" leader he was, still needed to have his faith strengthened by fellowship with others.

Today's Thoughts: _____

_____

_____

☐ **Today's Text: Romans 1:16-19** *(key v. 16)*

3 **Today's Truth:** The Gospel is the *power of God.* We rarely question that–until it comes to God's power to totally forgive us. Condemnation makes us feel like God might *try* to forgive us, but "His batteries could be too weak for such a large job."

Today's Thoughts: _____

_____

_____

☐ **Today's Text: Romans 1:20-32** *(key v. 20)*

4 **Today's Truth:** Though God is invisible to our physical eyes, He has emblazoned upon every horizon throughout the earth His signature of glory which proclaims: "I AM HERE!" He wants all to be saved if only they will seek Him.

Today's Thoughts: _____

_____

_____

☐ **Today's Text: Romans 2:1-4** *(key v. 1)*

5 **Today's Truth:**   A recipe for condemnation: judging others for doing things you yourself do! However, if we ongoingly forgive others, confess our sin, and repent earnestly, infinite grace is ours.

Today's Thoughts: _____

_____

_____

☐ **Today's Text: Romans 2:5-11** *(key v. 11)*

6 **Today's Truth:** There is no favoritism with God. So the chief issue is: if our lives are hidden with Christ (the *only* Favored One) in God, then we are *all favored* via Christ's righteousness–for He loves us all equally!

Today's Thoughts:_____

_____

_____

☐ **Today's Text: Romans 2:12-16** *(key v. 16)*

7 **Today's Truth:** Terrifying words: "when God will judge the secrets of men." But if our "secret sins" have all been exposed through confession and repentence, and they have been sent away as far as the east is from the west, then we can have confidence in the day of His appearing! Hallelujah!

Today's Thoughts: _____

_____

_____

☐ **Today's Text: Romans 2:17-29** *(key v. 29)*

8 **Today's Truth:** God's plea is for internal righteousness of heart, not outward religiousness. In the parable of the Pharisee and the tax collector in Lk. 18:10-14, the sinner who humbled himself and asked for mercy was justified before God.

Today's Thoughts: _____

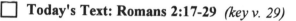

_____

☐ **Today's Text: Romans 3:1-8** *(key v. 4)*

9 **Today's Truth:** God is *true*. The Greek word, *alethes*, means: genuine, real, ideal. He is incapable of falsehood and is therefore absolutely faithful to keep all of His promises.

Today's Thoughts: _____

_____

_____

81

☐ **Today's Text: Romans 3:9-18** *(key v. 10)*

10 **Today's Truth:** The sooner we realize the full extent of the depravity of man–that is, our own hopeless state as sinners, the sooner we'll learn to seek God's righteousness and not our own. "Blessed are the poor in spirit " refers to those who recognize their spiritual poverty, and who trust in the Lord's resources instead of their own.

Today's Thoughts: ―――――――――――――
―――――――――――――――――――――――――
―――――――――――――――――――――――――

☐ **Today's Text: Romans 3:19-26** *(key v. 24)*

11 **Today's Truth:** "Redemption" is a power-packed word. The Greek term, *apolutrosis*, describes a master ransoming a slave, and freeing him from a yoke of bondage.

Today's Thoughts: ―――――――――――――
―――――――――――――――――――――――――
―――――――――――――――――――――――――

☐ **Today's Text: 3:27-31** *(key v. 27)*

12 **Today's Truth:** Although few of us may be tempted to approach God on the basis of our own righteousness, we often fall prey to an inverted form of that logic: based on our *un*righteousness, we feel unworthy to come to Him and be forgiven (cf. Heb. 4:16: "Let us come boldly . . .").

Today's Thoughts: ―――――――――――――
―――――――――――――――――――――――――
―――――――――――――――――――――――――

☐ **Today's Text: Romans 4:1-4** *(key v. 3)*

13 **Today's Truth:** Abraham's faith was *accounted*
to him for righteousness. The Greek term,
logidzomai, from which we get the English word
logic, means God "computed, calculated, summed
up, and reasoned" that Abraham was righteous
because of his faith (and even *that* was a gift.) After
all, based on God's eternal principles of redemption, it was only *logical.*

Today's Thoughts: _____ _____

_____

_____

☐ **Today's Text: Romans 4:5-10** *(key vv. 6-8)*

14 **Today's Truth:** In respect to categorizing sins,
we often think of murder and adultery as the all-
time "biggies." Nevertheless, David's sin in both of
these areas was forgiven and blotted out.

Today's Thoughts: _____

_____

_____

☐ **Today's Text: Romans 4:11-19** *(key vv. 17-18)*

15 **Today's Truth:** God's creative power is released
in "hopeless" situations when we simply believe His
Word rather than circumstances. Abraham's body
was dead to procreation, but today the nation of
Israel proves his "hopeless" circumstance was a lie.

Today's Thoughts: _____

_____

_____

83

☐ **Today's Text: Romans 4:20-25** *(key v. 25)*

16 **Today's Truth:** We *know* our sins are paid for because Jesus died on the Cross. We *know* we are justified before God because Jesus rose from the dead. So the next time you feel *un*justified, escort your doubts to the empty tomb. And celebrate.

Today's Thoughts: _____

_____

_____

☐ **Today's Text: Romans 5:1-5** *(key v. 5)*

17 **Today's Truth:** God's love: *agape*, conveys God's undefeatable benevolence and unconquerable goodwill wherein He always seeks His children's highest benefit no matter what weaknesses or failures they are struggling with.

Today's Thoughts: _____

_____

_____

☐ **Today's Text: Romans 5:6-11** *(key vv. 8-9)*

18 **Today's Truth:** It's a mind-boggler: when we were in our *worst* state–"still sinners"–Christ did the *most* for us. Now as His kids, how "much more then" shall we be saved to the utmost.

Today's Thoughts:_____

_____

_____

☐ **Today's Text: Romans 5:12-16** *(key vv. 14-15)*

19 **Today's Truth:** Even without our sinning in the likeness of Adam's transgression, just being *in Adam* results in the sentence of death through the universally inherited sin nature. Conversely, being *in Christ* is the "lock and seal" of life.

Today's Thoughts: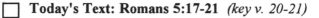

_____

_____

☐ **Today's Text: Romans 5:17-21** *(key v. 20-21)*

20 **Today's Truth:** Two actions of God's grace in our lives: *abounding* and *reigning*. One speaks of ample quantity–more than enough; the other speaks of ruling power through righteousness.

Today's Thoughts: _____

_____

_____

☐ **Today's Text: Romans 6:1-6** *(key v. 4)*

21 **Today's Truth:** Total identification with Christ! We can look at our heinous past sins and say, "Oh my–I'm dead meat!" And in Christ, that's exactly right. We're dead! That sinful man is dead. Now we can walk in confidence knowing that the "dead weight" of our past sins is gone; the new man created in Christ is alive!

Today's Thoughts: _____

_____

_____

☐ **Today's Text: Romans 6:7-11** *(key v. 11)*

22 **Today's Truth:** To reckon yourself dead to sin and alive unto God takes practice. *Reckon* means "consider it a fact." Even when you feel alive to sin and dead to God, God has a different judgment on the issue!

Today's Thoughts: ―――――――

――――――――――――――――――――――

――――――――――――――――――――――

☐ **Today's Text: Romans 6:12-16** *(key v. 16)*

23 **Today's Truth:** Since we are all "wired for sin," sin stands by ready to dominate us if we simply *present* ourselves to it. Give sin an inch, and it seeks to consume our lives. Instead, let's "tap in" to obedience, which leads to righteousness.

Today's Thoughts: ―――――――

――――――――――――――――――――――

――――――――――――――――――――――

☐ **Today's Text: Romans 6:17-23** *(key v. 19)*

24 **Today's Truth:** The more we yield ourselves to sin, the easier it is to keep sinning. But the same goes for righteousness. It, too, seeks to be our master.

Today's Thoughts: ―――――――

――――――――――――――――――――――

――――――――――――――――――――――

☐ **Today's Text: Romans 7:1-6** *(key v. 6)*

25 **Today's Truth:** Now, with our deliverance from the law established, God can deal with us as sons rather than as debtors. That certainly does not eliminate the issue of obedience, but now there's a loving family relationship in which obedience takes place.

Today's Thoughts: ————————————

————————————————————————

————————————————————————

☐ **Today's Text: Romans 7:7-12** *(key v. 12)*

26 **Today's Truth:** The Psalmist cries out, "I love Your law!" (Ps. 119) for it is a light to our feet. Yet though the law is perfect, it is totally powerless to help us obey it. We need a Savior.

Today's Thoughts: ————————————

————————————————————————

————————————————————————

☐ **Today's Text: Romans 7:13-19** *(key v. 19)*

27 **Today's Truth:** Thank you, Paul, for identifying with our struggles! His admission of personal struggle is not to give us license to sin (cf. 6:15-23!), but rather to encourage us that we're not alone in our battle for holiness.

Today's Thoughts:————————————

————————————————————————

————————————————————————

☐ **Today's Text: Romans 7:20-25** *(key v. 25)*

28

Today's Truth: Paul's cry of victory is not because the struggle ceases, but because of recognition that human strength is surpassed by the power of the Resurrected Christ!

Today's Thoughts: _____

_____

_____

☐ **Today's Text: Romans 8:1-11** *(key v. 2)*

29

Today's Truth: The law of the Spirit of life in Christ provides the assistance of Omnipotence for our victory. Our pilgrimage, however, requires that we ongoingly learn HOW to yield to, trust in, obey, and rest in God's Spirit—a discipline which may require a little more than one month for us to perfect!

Today's Thoughts: _____

_____

_____

☐ **Today's Text: Romans 8:12-23** *(key v. 18)*

30

Today's Truth: Such blessed assurance: whatever sufferings we know in life, the glory that shall come later *can't even be compared to them*—it's so far off the scale of measure!

Today's Thoughts: _____

_____

_____

☐ **Today's Text: Romans 8:24-39** *(key v. 37)*

31 Today's Truth: We are *more* than conquerors through Christ (as if being *mere* conquerors wasn't enough!) because of the content of all eight chapters preceding this verse. In the courtroom of heaven, picture the Father as the Judge, the Son as our Attorney, and the Holy Spirit as the Jury–not to mention the fact that we were acquitted long before this court came into session! Now here's a test:

What do the proclamations of Romans 8 work in your heart:

> *"confidence"* or
> *"CONFIDENCE!!!"* ?

Today's Thoughts: _____

_____
_____
_____
_____
_____

Additional Resources for Biblical Manhood. . .

BOOKS

A MAN'S STARTING PLACE

This first book in the "Power-to-Become" Book-Pak series is a study of how men become mature in Christ through relationships with God, their spouse, and with other men. It is available individually or with its companion audio tape. **Book only: AMSP $3.95
Book & Tape: BP01 $7.95**

NEWBORN

This book outlines the basic elements in a growing life with Jesus and discusses the believer's relationship to God, how the Bible can help in one's spiritual journey, types of baptism, and the need for spending time with other believers. **NBN $ 3.95**

DAYBREAK: Walking With Christ Every Day

Transforms generalized exhortations about "daily devotions" into a workable, non-legalistic set of specifics as to how the earnest believer can develop a fulfilling devotional prayer life. **DBK $ 2.95**

PRAYERPATH

Pastor Hayford takes the reader step by step along the pathway of prayer, examining the things Jesus taught about how to live and grow in vital faith, as well as how to pray for spiritual breakthrough at a global dimension. **PRP $ 3.95**

SPIRIT-FILLED:
The Overflowing Power Of The Holy Spirit

Practical instruction on the Person and Power of the Spirit, teaching the enablement and resources of spiritual gifts and graces. Encourages the reader to open to the fullness of the Spirit of Christ, and shows how to maintain wisdom and balance in daily Spirit-filled living. **SFL $ 3.95**

TAKING HOLD OF TOMORROW

The practical principles of "Possessing the Promised Land," found in the story of Joshua, encourage the reader to move forward and actively take hold of God's promises in life. This Angel Award winning book teaches the believer about spiritual warfare, submission, personal holiness, and obedience. *(Regularly $12.95)* **THT $ 9.95**

This same subject is presented in an 8-tape audio album and in a series of 4 videotapes.

Audio SC130 $34   Video PYTVS $65

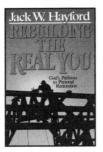

REBUILDING THE REAL YOU

Just as Nehemiah went to Jerusalem with all the provisions he would need to rebuild the walls of the city, so the Holy Spirit comes with all that is needed to restore a broken personality. *(Regularly $8.95)* **RRY02 $7.95**

The same subject is presented in 11 audio tapes or 6 videotapes.   **Audio SC046 $49.00**
Video RTWVS $99.00

AUDIO CASSETTE MINI-ALBUMS (2 tapes)

Honest to God	**SC122**	**$8**
Redeeming Relationships for Men & Women	**SC177**	**$8**
Why Sex Sins Are Worse Than Others	**SC179**	**$8**
How God Uses Men	**SC223**	**$8**
A Father's Approval	**SC225**	**$8**
Resisting the Devil	**SC231**	**$8**
The War in Your Life and World	**SC367**	**$8**
How to Recession-Proof Your Home	**SC369**	**$8**
Safe Sex!	**SC448**	**$8**
The Leader Jesus Trusts	**SC461**	**$8**

AUDIO CASSETTE ALBUMS (# of tapes)

Cleansed for the Master's Use (3)	**SC377**	**$13**
Becoming God's Man (4)	**SC457**	**$17**
Fixing Family Fractures (4)	**SC217**	**$17**
The Power of Blessing (4)	**SC395**	**$17**

Men's Seminars 1990-91 (10)	**MSEM**	**$42**
Premarital Series (12)	**PM02**	**$50**
A Family Encyclopedia (24)	**SC233**	**$99**

VHS VIDEO ALBUMS

Why Sex Sins Are Worse Than Others	**WSSV**	**$19**
Divorce and the People of God	**DIVV**	**$19**
Earthly Search for a Heavenly Father	**ESFV**	**$19**

Add 15% for shipping and handling.
California residents add 8.25% sales tax.

Request your _free_ Resource Catalog.

**Call Living Way Ministries Resources
at (818) 779-8180 or (800) 776-8180.**